Visiting Bordeaux

ALBERT RÈCHE and PHILIPPE PRÉVÔT

Photographs by Pascal Moulin
Translated by Angela Cadwell

ÉDITIONS SUD OUEST

Bordeaux, 2,500 years of history

Recent archaeological digs have shown that the Gauls had a settlement in Bordeaux in the 7th century B.C.

Three centuries later, a Celtic tribe, the Bituriges-Vivisci, crossed the Garonne and settled on the left bank of the major waterway, beside a stream transformed by two confluents into a veritable little river, later called the Devèze. Redeveloped straight away by these new settlers, the mouth of this river provided a sheltered harbour in the middle of an area crisscrossed by numerous streams that flowed down from the moors and out into the Garonne which described a crescent shape at this point. The Bituriges-Vivisci settled on these strips of land in the middle of the marshes and turned the Garonne into a "Celtic river" by taking control of the tin route. The mineral, which was vital for the manufacture of bronze, was shipped from the British Isles by sea and taken upriver to a Frankish port with a mysterious name that has kept its secret to this day – Burdigala.

The Biturige warriors (their name meant "kings of the world"), who were then ensured of a monopoly on the tin trade with the Mediterranean and Narbonne areas, found that they were skilful tradesmen and, when Lutèce grew up on the banks of the Seine, Burdigala became an "emporion" or market town, according to the Greek geographer Strabo. Bordeaux, which owed its existence to commerce, was destined to be a trading centre for more than two thousand years.

Thus it was that, when Julius Caesar drew up a list of the Gallic tribes who had sent reinforcements to Vercingétorix in an effort to fight off the Roman invader, the Bituriges-Vivisci were noticeable by their absence – no doubt they already considered war as being prejudicial to trade! It was, after all, better to maintain peaceful relations with good customers who were also suppliers inasmuch as the ancestors of the people of Bordeaux imported a much-appreciated Mediterranean wine from Campania. However, they quickly abandoned this wine once they had discovered a type of vine that stood up to the maritime climate, the *biturica*, the forerunner of the vines in the Gironde and the source of Bordeaux' wealth.

From the top of the Pey-Berland Tower, there is a 360° view of the city with its grey slate and pink tile roofs.

THE GALLIEN PALACE (Palais Gallien)

This 15,000-seat amphitheatre built in the 2dn century was believed by the mediaeval population to have been a palace built by Charlemagne for a beautiful Saracen woman named Galliène. Hence its name. Its ruins provided shelter for criminals and prostitutes and rumour had it that witches met here, until one of the town's mayors used it as a source of building stone during the French Revolution! Its stones were used in the housing nearby.

GALLIEN PALACE
Open from 1st June to 30 September
14 pm – 7 pm
Rue du Docteur-Albert-Barraud
Tel.: 05 56 00 66 00

Bordeaux, 25,000 years of history

Burdigala, "little Rome"

With *pax romana* came the expansion of Bordeaux. Using the standard rules of Roman town planning, the occupying forces in the Bituriges-Viviscis' community as far back as the first half of the 1st century B.C. traced out the two main roads in the town. The north-south road, or *cardo*, corresponds to what we now know as the Rue Sainte-Catherine extending as far as the Place des Quinconces, while the east-west road, or *decumanus*, now lies under the Cours du Chapeau-Rouge and Cours de l'Intendance. At the junction of these two roads was the forum (now the Place de la Comédie).

A network of parallel streets spread out from this point, finally covering some one hundred and twenty-five hectares, the area of the 3rd-century town that had become the capital of Aquitaine. This was "Little Rome", a cosmopolitan city which had the privilege of seeing its governor, Tetricus, proclaimed emperor and don the imperial purple in his own town. Bordeaux was then a prosperous and open town of 25,000 inhabitants.

At the end of the 3rd century, people protect themselves with tall ramparts. By then, the inhabitants numbered no more than between 12,000 and 15,000 out of an original population of between 25,000 and 30,000 thousand. The ruins of temples, monuments and opulent mansions were used to build the walls of the castrum which limited the town to some thirty hectares between the Garonne to the east and the Rue des Ramparts to the west. On the north side, the present Cours de l'Intendance and Cours du Chapeau-Rouge have replaced the moats that once surrounded these 4th-century ramparts; the same is true of the Cours d'Alsace-Lorraine to the south.

The walls, whose great height was mentioned in the works of Ausone, the first poet of the Bordeaux region, enabled the town to withstand successive waves of invasion by Vandals, Visigoths, Franks, Saracens and Vikings between the 5th and 9th centuries, after the respite during the 4th century that had given the town an opportunity to regain its former splendour. The people of Bordeaux were to seek refuge in this castrum for 700 years.

The 7th century was marked by the organisation of the walled town into parishes. This followed a meeting by the first Christians, in a place left to fall into ruin. They had been represented at the Council of Arles in 314 A.D. by Bishop Orientalis whose name would seem to suggest that the new religion had been imported into the area by travellers.

The basilica church dedicated to St. Seurin, the cradle of Christianity in Bordeaux.

Burdigala, "little Rome"

ST SEURIN'S CHURCH (église Saint-Seurin)

St. Seurin's was built beside an earlier church which no longer exists but which, in the 3rd century A.D, was used by Bordeaux' first Christians. Three centuries later, the basilica church containing the relics of St. Seurin, patron saint of Bordeaux, enjoyed considerable privileges. The various buildings erected on this site over the years were all destroyed as a result of the invasions that rocked Bordeaux, a town that never had any defensive walls.

By 1100, only the porch and crypt remained. The chevet, transept, part of the nave and side aisles, the western bell tower and the square tower on the south side all date from the 12th century. The nave as we see it today dates from the 13th century, the south door from the 14th, the chapel on the left of the chancel from the 15th and the south porch from the 16th. As to the West Front, which was rebuilt in 1830 in the Neo-Romanesque style, it hides the original porch in which visitors can admire the craft of 11th-century sculptors in the pillars and capitals (in particular, "Abraham's sacrifice" and "snakes and animals devouring each other"). Their work highlights the mediocrity of the 19th-century decorations on the West Front itself. The other door, on the south side, a 13th-century portal that was clumsily restored in 1844, is preceded by a vast polygonal Renaissance porch containing the arching of the splendid original doorway with tympani bearing a variety of characters and subjects e.g. "The Last Judgement", "The Resurrection of the Dead", "The Holy Women at the Tomb", apostles, bishops etc.

The interior of the basilica includes a chancel that is smaller than the original. In it is an altar above a 5th-century sarcophagus containing the relics of St. Seurin and St. Amand. Behind it are thirty-two 16th-century stalls decorated with satirical, and highly picturesque, subjects. There is also a 15th-century Bishop's Throne, a veritable piece of lacework in stone, and, opposite it, fourteen alabaster bas-reliefs.

The basilica includes several chapels, including the Chapel of Our Lady of the Rose (1427) containing the altar consecrated by Archbishop Pey-Berland and its reredos of 12 alabaster bas-reliefs depicting scenes from the life of the Virgin Mary (15th century). In St. Veronica's Chapel, where the font now stands, there is a beautiful 17th-century bronze basin.

The original crypt, consisting of three narrow, dark aisles separated by marble columns with Gallo-Roman capitals, is paved with 13th-century glazed tiles. It contains a number of magnificent sarcophagi dating from the 6th and 7th centuries, including one

The archaeology museum in St. Seurin's Church.

known as "St. Fort's Tomb". The veneration in which the people of Bordeaux held this particular saint eventually surpassed their love of St. Seurin, for legend had it that he "gave strength" to children brought to him!

The tombs in the crypt, beneath which experts have recently found an older building, serve as reminders of the fact that, next to the church, there used to be the famous graveyard praised in the *Song of Roland*.

THE ARCHAEOLOGICAL DIG AT ST. SEURIN'S

It was in 1910 that the first archaeological dig was carried out, on the south side of St. Seurin's Church. It revealed a vast Christian cemetery with graves laid one on top of the other, dating from the 4th to the 18th centuries. Legend has it that this old graveyard, which was the most famous cemetery in Christendom in the Middle Ages along with the Alyscamps in Arles, was consecrated by Christ and His saints. Pilgrims heading for Santiago de Compostela came to pray here, kneeling beside the stone coffins that had been exhumed. They also listened to the tales of Charlemagne's knights who were buried here after the Battle of Roncevalles. Roland's horn was also a much venerated object. The archaeological dig revealed a set of walls forming small constructions from various periods, built one beside the other. They included tombs decorated with frescoes (parts of them still intact) and amphora-graves of very young children.

BASILIQUE SAINT-SEURIN
Place des Martyrs-
de-la-Résistance
Tel. : 05 56 48 56 42

SITE ARCHÉOLOGIQUE
DE SAINT-SEURIN
Place des Martyrs-
de-la-Résistance
Open from 1st June to 30h September, 2 pm – 7 pm
Tel. : 05 56 00 66 00

The cradle of local christianity

Outwith the town was the suburb of Saint-Seurin, the cradle of Christianity in the Bordeaux region, where the first believers gathered in their cathedral, St. Stephen's, which was quickly replaced by another church built alongside the original in the 6th century to receive the body of one Severinus, later St. Seurin, protector of the town and a person so highly-venerated that everybody wanted to be buried near him. And during the days of the great pilgrimages to Compostella, the graveyard round St. Seurin's Basilica became the most famous cemetery in the whole of the Christian world, with the Alyscamps in Arles. Indeed, it was said that Charlemagne's valiant knights were buried there and that the oliphant used by Roland in Roncesvalles was laid on St. Seurin's tomb.

The basilica's canons, who benefitted from this religious fervour, received gifts of land and money which made them powerful lords until the French Revolution. Some of their property included a right of asylum and the canons continually showed a fiercely-held spirit of independence, standing up to the canons from St. Andrew's cathedral and the members of the town council; this led to many a conflict. A veritable village grew up around the basilica, attracting craftsmen who wanted to rid themselves of the constraints placed upon them by the corporations. In the 18th century, they were mostly weavers, dyers, potters, and building workers. The latter were highly sought after when, having achieved great wealth through trade with the overseas colonies, Bordeaux was smitten by feverish property investment programmes.

Let's go back again in time, though, to July 1453. The English were defeated in Castillon and finally lost the last of their claims to the Kingdom of France. The One Hundred Years' War drew to a close and, in October, Bordeaux became French again. But not always willingly for its population realised that there was a strong possibility that it would lose the privileges it had managed to gain from a monarch on a throne far across the seas. Charles VII, the reconquering king, ordered the building of two fortresses, the Château Trompette to the north of the town and the Fort du Hâ to the west. Their purpose was twofold – to protect the town against a hypothetical return by the English and to keep in check any locals with pro-English tendencies. The local administration underwent a purge to ensure that it would thereafter be pro-French. With 1462 came the setting up of the High Court.

Eleanor or the advantages of the One Hundred Years's war

When, after the raids carried out by the Viking pirates, the power of the Carolingian Empire began to crumble away and, shortly afterwards, the Dukes of Aquitaine succeeded the Dukes of Gascony, a fortress topped by a keep was erected in the southeastern corner of the ramparts near the river. This was the dark mass of the ducal residence, the Château de l'Ombrière (a street name is a continuing reminder of its erstwhile existence), which, on July 1137, was the setting for the marriage breakfast of the young Duchess of Aquitaine, Eleanor, and the future King Louis VII of France. Fifteen years later, the couple's divorce seriously changed the destiny of Bordeaux and the region as a whole: Eleanor then remarried, her second husband being a Plantagenet, Henry II. By this action, she turned Aquitaine into English territory and Bordeaux into a prosperous city, thanks to the business links between the banks of the R.Garonne and those of the Thames.

This was the era of the wine trade. The English appreciated the beverage and, every year, awaited the completion of the grape harvest with as much impatience as they now wait for Beaujolais Nouveau. As soon as the grapes had been pressed, the "wine fleet". Froissart tells us that it comprised some "200 single-sailed ships" ready to set off under escort. "The one thing that was to ruin France as a whole", writes Camille Jullian, "was to provide wealth and happiness for Bordeaux : the One Hundred Years' War took it to the pinnacle of its splendour." Indeed, the people of the Bor-

HOLYROOD CHURCH (église Sainte-Croix)

Once the minster of the Benedictine abbey, the sumptuous Romanesque West Front of the Holy Cross Church, which was built between the 10th and the 13th Centuries, was recomposed in the 19th century by the architect Paul Abadie. The interior, which has ribbed vaulting, contains some interesting Gothic capitals.

The nave has five bays, two side aisles, a transept, and a nine-sided apse preceded by a bay and two apsidal chapels. Between the south aisle and the transept, there is a Romanesque capital ("Abraham's sacrifice"). Two more Romanesque capitals can be seen further on, "Daniel in the lions' den" and "Jesus amidst the Pharisees".

St. Monmolin's Chapel contains two fine 17th-century paintings representing St. Benedict and St. Scholastica, and a 16th-century bas-relief showing the Last Supper. It originally formed the top of the font. Opposite it is a gilded wooden statue dating from the 18th century which was much venerated and known as Our Lady of Consolation.

The minster was originally part of the Benedictine abbey. The monks settled in what was then an isolated spot in the 7th century, far from any town, and it was in their abbey that, c. 679 A.D., St. Monmolin, Abbot of Fleury-sur-Loire, died when he was passing through Bordeaux. Ravaged by the Vikings, the Benedictine monastery was destroyed but the chapel containing the saint's relics was left standing. Two centuries later, the monastery came back into existence and its church is thought to have been built in the late 11th century, between 1091 and 1120. When the new sacristy was laid out c. 1893, digs uncovered a number of stone tombs from the Merovingian period, one of them a very ornate piece.

deaux region obtained a number of considerable privileges – freedom from taxation for the wine they exported, a prohibition on the shipping of "foreign wines" (i.e. foreign to Bordeaux) downstream from the Garonne and out to sea until 11th November or even Christmas so that the burghers of Bordeaux had time to sell their stocks before the winter storms set in, for only young wine was appreciated at a time when nobody knew how to store it. Any wine from outwith the Bordeaux region had to wait for spring, when the wine fleet returned. For wine that had been stored since Christmas in a distant suburb of the town called the Chartrons.

The West Front of Holyrood Church (église Sainte-Croix), built circa 1150 but with extensive alterations dating from 1860. The layout and carvings are reminiscent of the Romanesque architecture seen in and around Angoulême.

ST. ANDREW'S CATHEDRAL (cathédrale Saint-André)

St. Andrew's Cathedral took four hundred years to build, from the 12th to the 16th centuries. It consists of a nave 124 metres long and 23 metres tall and a West Front that is simply a bare wall because it was built against the town walls. The north side, on the other hand, includes the 13th-century Royal Doorway decorated with numerous carvings. It used to open onto the courtyard of the Archbishop's Palace. It has now been. The door has now been walled up but it was once used by the highest dignitaries in the land e.g. François I, Emperor Charles V, and, later, Louis XIII and Anne of Austria when they were married in Bordeaux.

Beyond it, in the ambulatory, are seven chapels, one of which contains an alabaster statue of Our Lady of the Nave (16th century). It was here that the governors used to be sworn in. There are a number of bas-reliefs, also made of alabaster (15th century) and, beside the chancel, a statue of the Virgin Mary and St. Anne (16th century). At the end of the nave, note the chancel and the wrought-iron screens made by Blaise Charlut in the 18th century. As to the carved wooden stalls, they were made by Tournier and date from 1690.

The north door of the transept (14th century) has a wonderful tympanum showing, from top to bottom, Christ in triumph, the Ascension and the Last Supper. The south door is older, dating from the late 13th century, but it is in a very poor state of repair and its statues have been damaged. The cathedral treasure includes a number of paintings by Jordaens and José Ribera, Italian primitives dating from the 14th and 15th Centuries, a collection of illuminated manuscripts from the Middle Ages and Renaissance period, and a set of Flemish and Spanish vestments made in the 15th and 17th Centuries.

ST. ANDREW'S CATHEDRAL
8,30 am – 11,30 am; 2 pm – 5,30 pm
Closed Sundays afternoons
Place Pey-Berland
Open all year

THE PEY-BERLAND TOWER (tour Pey-Berland)

The Pey-Berland Tower stands on its own but is the bell tower for the cathedral. It was named after the archbishop who is said to have commissioned its construction and laid the foundation stone on 6th October 1440. Sold in 1793 and turned into a factory making shot for huntsmen, which it remained until 1850, then bought by Cardinal Donnet and restored, the tower acquired an eleven-tonne bell. The top of the tower was missing; in 1863, it was given a huge gilded copper statue of Our Lady of Aquitaine which has recently been restored.

PEY-BERLAND TOWER
10 am – 18 pm
Closed Mondays
Place Pey-Berland
Tel.: 05 56 81 26 25

Eleanor or the advantages of the One Hundred Years's war

THE GREAT BELL (la Grosse Cloche)

The Great Bell, which was the town belfry as far back as the 15th century when it stood between the parish church of St. Ely (église Saint-Eloi) and the now non-existent *oustau de villa* (i.e. Town Hall), has rung out the passage of time for the people of Bordeaux for many a long year. After the alterations carried out in the 16th and 18th Centuries (the clock dates from 1759), this austere construction stands 133 ft. high. It consists of two inter-connected round towers dominated by the golden leopard at the top. It replaced the old St. Ely Gate that opened onto the 13th-century ramparts and was used by pilgrims on their way to Santiago de Compostella.

Originally, the St. Ely Gate, also known as the Saint-James Gate, had four round towers to which another two were added in the 13th century. It was only one storey high. Successive alterations carried out between the 15th and 17th Centuries completely changed the original appearance of the gate, which became a belfry after the belltower used by the town crier for communal proclamations was added in the 15th century.

There was another alteration in 1561 when the bell, which had been removed on the orders of King Henri II and smashed to punish the locals for their revolt in 1548, was finally replaced, to the immense joy of the good people of Bordeaux.

A further alteration followed the fire of 1755 when the pepper-pot towers were given crenelations and a campanile.

In the centre of the 18th-century wrought-iron railing across the archway containing the bell is the town's coat-of-arms while, on the north side, there are grimacing 15th-century gargoyles. Below them are inscriptions engraved on black marble dating from 1592. As to the clock, built in 1759 by the astronomer, Larroque, it replaced the one dating from 1567 which had been made by Raymond Sudre.

The belfry and bell can still be seen on Bordeaux' coat-of-arms.

OPPOSITE

The Great Bell, once the belfry on the mediaeval Town Hall, used to tower above the Saint-Eloi district. Above the lantern tower is a weathervane representing the English leopard, the emblem of the Province of Guyenne of which Bordeaux was the capital.

Cast in June 1775 in the Turmel foundry, the bells weighs 7,800 kg and is 2 metres in height and diameter.

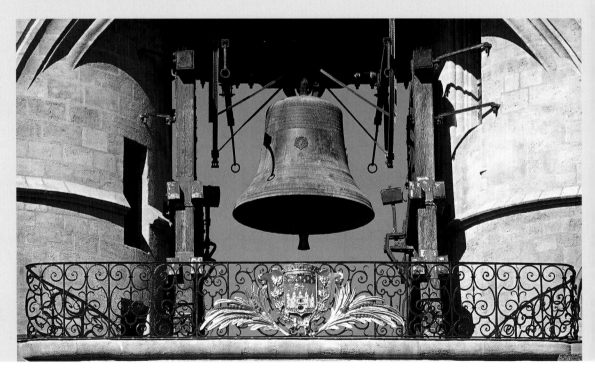

Eleanor or the advantages of the One Hundred Years's war

Wine, a source of wealth

This privilege, which the locals managed to maintain until 1776, gave them an easy market for the wine production that they then expanded by planting vineyards further afield. The 14th century was Bordeauxs golden age, a time of wealth and prosperity not seen again until the 18th century, when trade flourished with the Isles. Edward, Prince of Wales, the Black Prince, was triumphant and it was said of him that he was the most magnificent lord of his day.

As to the town, it had shed its Gallo-Roman yoke. It expanded southwards beyond the present Cours d'Alsace-Lorraine and new districts were built – the market district or "lou mercat" (Place Ferdinand-Lafargue), the Rousselle District near the river, where salt, cod, sardines and herring were landed and where the merchants had their warehouses and mansions built, while the wealthiest burghers had their "oustaus" built in the Rue Neuve.

This was also a period of veritable feuds, like the one opposing Montaigus and Capulets, between the town's rich families e.g. the Solers and Coloms, rival factions seeking power within the community, for since the early 13th century the town had obtained a measure of freedom with government by aldermen (who swore loyalty to the town) and a mayor. Around the St-Eloi District which housed the town council offices, town hall, and main church, there was new hustle and bustle, increased by the establishment of several convents and monasteries situated outwith the new walls whose moat corresponded to what we now know as the Cours Victor-Hugo.

For centuries, there had been protection round the market, the veritable heart of the town, the business centre for anything connected with harbour activities, and the Saint-Eloi District. Yet the increasing population and the presence of monasteries and convents on the outskirts of the town made it necessary for the town council to commission the costly construction of a third wall, the 14th-century ramparts.

Nowadays, if you want to follow it along its 3-mile length, you simply set off from the rostral columns at one end of the Place des Quinconces, walk along the river to the Holy Cross Church, then go up the Cours de la Marne and the Cours Aristide-Briand. Beyond St.Eulalie's Church, take the Rue Maréchal-Joffre and the Rue des Remparts, then the Rue de la Vieille-Tour and the Rue Condillac, cross the Place Tourny and, finally, walk right across the centre of the Place des Quinconces back to the river bank.

To the north, these new walls protected Dominicans and, later, Recollects; to the

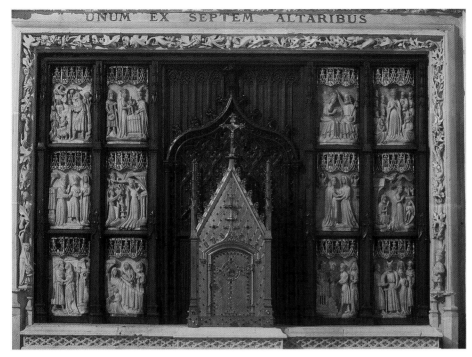

UNUM EX SEPTEM ALTARIBUS

After the merger of the dynasties of the Duchy of Aquitaine and the Crown of England, there was an increase in the imports of alabaster carvings made in London, Nottingham and York. The examples in St. Seurin's Church, depicting the lives of St. Martial and St. Seurin, are exquisitely carved.

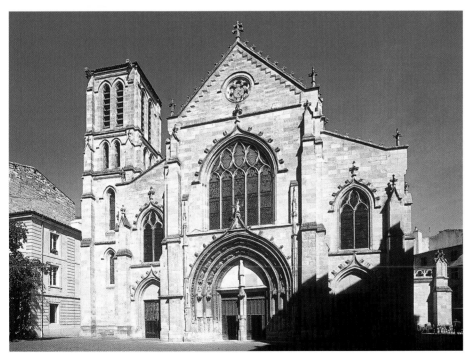

St. Peter's Church (église Saint-Pierre). The foundations of this 15th-century building lie partly over the remains of the old river port. The West Front of the church was extensively restored in the 19th century.

south, they afforded protection to Carmelites, Augustinians, and members of the Order of St. Clare, all of whom attracted blacksmiths and carpenters (or "fustiers") whose trades live on in street names of the Rue des Faures and the Rue de la Fusterie in the parish of St. Michael. Goldsmiths and coffer-makers lived in the St.Peter District, in the Rue des Argentiers and the Rue des Bahutiers, while the Carmelite Convent near the centre of the town, soon to be dominated by its belfry, the so-called Great Bell, was the home of the University founded by Archbishop Pey Berland in 1441, with the Pope's blessing of course.

ST. MICHAEL'S TOWER (la flèche Saint-Michel)
Like the one on the cathedral, the belltower of St. Michael's Church is an isolated construction, some 49 ft. away from the main building. To the people of Bordeaux, it is known as the "spire". It is the tallest building in the south-west of France and has stood at over 370 ft. since the 15th century. It was used for the first Chappe telegraph and, for many years, its basement attracted visitors who came to seem a rather macabre spectacle – mummies presented by a picturesque guide. A 22-bell peal mounted in 1865 rings melodiously out every 15 minutes.

ST. MICHAEL'S TOWER
Place Canteloup
Open every day from 1st June to 30th September
14 pm – 19 pm
Tel.: 05 56 00 66 00

The Renaissance

For a while, shipments of wine to England declined, replaced by woad from the "land of plenty" around Toulouse, and, with trade in salt fish, this provided a source of wealth for a family named Eyquem. The profits they acquired in the Rousselle District enabled them to purchase an aristocratic property in Montaigne and a position as Counsellor to the High Court for one of their descendents who was non other than the philosopher Michel de Montaigne. He was appointed Mayor of Bordeaux in 1581, one year after the publication of the first edition of his *Essays*.

The wine trade picked up again, followed by high-sea fishing off Newfoundland. Soon, trade with the colonies was, in its turn, to provide new wealth for the town. Trade with the Antilles led to the creation of a sugar industry in Bordeaux, while exchanges of wine and English wool increased. New markets opened up in Scandinavia, Flanders, Spain and Portugal. The late 16th and early 17th centuries saw the arrival of Dutch merchants and ships from the United Provinces.

THE CAILHAU GATE

This gate was built in 1495 to commemorate the conquest of Naples and the victory at Fornova in which the nobility of Bordeaux played a part. It has machicolations and pointed roofs with dormer windows and lantern towers. On the side overlooking Place du Palais is the French coat-of-arms; on the side overlooking the quays, the statue of Charles VIII flanked by St. John, patron saint of the *"jurade"* or Town Council, and by Cardinal d'Epinay, Archbishop of Bordeaux who took part in the Battle of Fornova. The ornateness of the gate's architecture shows a clear desire for decorative detail even though the machicolations and slit windows give the gate a defensive role.

PORTE CAILHAU
Place du Palais
Open every day from 1st June to 30th September
14 pm – 19 pm. Tel. : 05 56 00 66 00

The remains of Fort Hâ (seen from the top of the Pey-Berland Tower) built on the orders of King Charles VII. The Minims and Englishmen's Towers are now encased by the buildings of the Magistrates' Court, a modern architectural design by Richard Rogers.

The Tax Revolt

When the Fronde Revolt broke out, Bordeaux was one of the rebel towns. It had already protested against fiscal measures (it seems to be a characteristic of Bordeaux!) but the Ormée, a veritable revolution that was specific to this rebellious community, created a particularly bitter situation. The red flag was hoisted on the tower of St. Michael's Church and, for more than seven months, Bordeaux was ruled by the leaders of the sedition. Twenty-five years later, there was another outbreak of anger when a question of taxation led Louis XIV to consider the town and its population as enemies of the throne and to repress the revolt by means of a veritable military occupation. The riots of 1675 led to increased surveillance of the rebellious locals and the setting up of Fort Louis, in the working-class district of Sainte-Croix. In addition, the Fort du Hâ was refurbished and the Château Trompette given extra fortifications. The king also ordered that all adjacent buildings should be razed to the ground (300 houses were demolished, including the fine Renaissance mansions in the Cours du Chapeau-Rouge) along with one of the only two Roman remains – the Tutelle Pillars, believed by some to be a temple and by others to have been the forum. One hundred years later, the site was selected for the Grand Theatre. And the Château Trompette, whose cannons were trained on the town, was justifiably described by Camille Jullian as an "emblem of a master's might and a town's captivity". It was a town that was thereafter held in check by three fortresses, two of which did not finally disappear until the 19th century. A few traces of the Fort du Hâ still remain today.

(ÉGLISE SAINT-BRUNO)

Cardinal François de Sourdis had facilitated the establishment of a Carthusian monastery in the 17th century, on the marshes on the outskirts of the town. Its foundation had been made possible thanks to a give from a monk named Blaise de Gascq and it marked the return to Bordeaux of an Order which had first arrived in the town in 1381 when, as a result of the One Hundred Years' War, it had been forced to flee its community in Périgord and resettle on the banks of the Garonne, on a stretch of wasteland to which it gave its name (Chartrons).

The monastery was set up in 1611 and, on 29th March 1620, its chapel (by then a church) was consecrated by the community's protector, the Cardinal. It was an austere church dedicated to St. Bruno. It has a nave 150 ft long containing a number of superb works of art, many of which were commissioned by Cardinal de Sourdis from Bernini (father and son).

St. Bruno's Church was pillaged during the French Revolution but it nevertheless retained the frescoes by Berinzago and Gonzales and a fine portrait of St. Bruno (17th century). The reredos in the chancel is decorated with marble taken from the Turks (they intended to take it to Mecca). On each side of the altar are statues by Bernini. The reredos behind the High Altar is decorated with an *Assumption* by Philippe de Champaigne (1673). To the left of the chancel, is the Sourdis family tomb (1691).

The famous Carthusian Gardens (jardin des Chartreux) which was also laid out on land reclaimed from the marshes, once drew the admiration of visitors for its design and its decoration. From the French Revolution onwards, it became the city's main cemetery.

(ÉGLISE SAINT-PAUL)

Once a Jesuit church called St. François-Xavier's and consecrated in 1696, it became St. Paul's Church in 1791 and is a small copy of the Gesù in Rome (the church was given a bell-tower in 1855).

Its altar, flanked by marble columns supporting a canopy, comprises two magnificent pieces of sculpture by Guillaume Coustou (1744-48), the *Apotheosis of St. Francis* and a marble tabernacle. It is interesting to compare this church to Notre-Dame.

NOTRE-DAME CHURCH (église Notre-Dame)

This Jesuit-style church designed by Michel du Plessy is a fine example of 17th-century architecture. Its single barrel-vaulted nave highlights the elegance of the balustrade and wrought ironwork in the chancel. It is usual to consider it as having a worldly charm and François Mauriac asserted that it was a "harmonious and moderate church, warm in winter, a place to which those who succeed in establishing for themselves a life on earth that provides all the creature comforts, come to ensure that eternity will give them as much pleasure".

THE PICHON MANSION (hôtel Pichon)

The Pichon Mansion (1610-1614) on Cours de l'Intendance lost some of its most attractive features at the turn of the century when it was turned into a department store. Yet despite this, it has retained its caryatids and the windows from which Louis XIV, who once stayed there, was able to see the crowds gathering to acclaim him, in particular when he returned from a visit to the vineyards of the Médoc belonging to the President Pichon, Baron of Longueville.

This residence, at 71 Rue du Loup, was built at the end of Louis XIII's reign by architect Pierre Léglise for the widow of the Counsellor to the Parliament, Pierre de Ragueneau. After being the toll gate for many years, it housed the offices of the Municipal Archives in 1939. The architecture is attractive on the façade and in the gallery and 18th-century balustrade linking the two wings of the building. Beneath the carriage entrance, with its undulating vaulting, there is a superb wisteria which is a constant source of delight for passers-by, especially in the spring when it is a profusion of strongly-scented blossoms. It is thought to be one of the oldest wisterias in the region.

COURS DU CHAPEAU-ROUGE

In the 18th century, this public promenade used to run along the slope in front of Castle Trompette.

Public promenades have long been a feature of Bordeaux, predating the Public Park. In the early 18th century, there were three public promenades for the pleasure of the people - the gardens round the Archbishop's Palace (now the Town Hall gardens), the Sainte-Eulalie platform known as L'Ormée and the avenues along the old "Tanners' Moat", now Cours Victor-Hugo. Since the moat no longer served any useful purpose, it was gradually filled in and replaced by tree-lined avenues which led to the town's layout being compared to "a nobleman's park" (Camille Jullian).

The finest of all the promenades was designed by Tourny in 1744. Four rows of young elms and Dutch limes formed a long ring of shade. Two rows of trees on Cours des Fossés-du-Chapeau-Rouge extended the promenade down to the banks of the river. Now, 250 years later, the trees are more or less in their original positions, as if the 18th century had been brought back to life.

"The town is ringed by an avenue almost three thousand paces long, planted with two rows of trees, forming the most agreeable promenade for the general public. The middle of the avenue is paved and has the added advantage of being suitable for carriages." *Guide de l'étranger à Bordeaux*, 1785.

New blood from the North

Outside the town walls, another suburb gradually developped, dating from a later period than the St. Seurin District. At the height of the One Hundred Years' War, a group of Carthusian monks from Périgord sought refuge in Bordeaux, in a marshy spot on the banks of the R. Garonne where the so-called "foreign" wines were stored when temporarily prohibited from entering the town. The monks soon set off for another destination, leaving their name to the suburb that had grown up around their monastery – the Chartrons District. In the early 17th century, the marshes were drained and, along the river, wine and spirits stores, warehouses and mansions were built for merchants from Flanders, the towns in the Hanseatic League, England and Ireland. This influx of foreign influence was to have a profound effect on the character of the town. The foreigners finally became an integral part of it, blending into its population but, at the same time, bringing an injection of new blood.

In fact, the 17th century was marked by a major project to control the marshes that crossed the town before disappearing below the waters of the Garonne, making Bordeaux "a town of fevers and malaria" where epidemics were much more serious than in any other large community. The locals remembered the plague that caused the death of 14,000 people in Bordeaux in 1585 out of a total population of approximately 35,000 and caused the Mayor, Michel de Montaigne, to flee his town. When, during the first three decades of the 17th century, a Flemish expert, Conrad Gaussen, drained the Chartrons District, Archbishop François de Sourdis drained the marshland in the west of the town to build a Carthusian convent next to St. Bruno's Church.

THE PAVE DES CHARTRONS

The present Cours Xavier-Arnozan was originally the famous Pavé des Chartrons. Changed into a tree-lined promenade, this has been the site, since the second half of the 18th century, of the houses that were "the pride and wealth of the upper middle classes", Bordeaux's shipowners and wine merchants. This is a street of unique character, with its austere elegance and the forceful architecture of the Laclotte brothers as shown in the group of Louis XV and Louis XVI houses decorated with balconies full of wrought iron arabesques on squinches. It is, in fact, a perfect example of an architectural style that had reached its climax at that time.

Originally, the Pavé des Chartrons was no more than a muddy lane running round Château Trompette and leading to the Chartrons District. It was then known as the Chemin de la Fausse-Braye. When Tourny commissioned the park and Grande Allée (now Cours de Verdun), he had the Fausse-Braye paved and it became a promenade. This, in turn, increased the value of the land along it opposite the bank on which the fortress was built. Property speculation was rife and the land was subdivided into lots, in particular on the former site of the old Mitchell glassworks founded in 1711 by an Irishman who had come to Bordeaux "to make glass suitable for the manufacture of English-style bottles". After the Restoration of the Monarchy, when Château-Trompette was demolished, the land on the south side of the Pavé des Chartrons became covered with private residences.

The Golden Age of a town made wealthy by colonial trade

The 18th century provided Bordeaux with its second golden age. Wine had formed the basis of the region's wealth in the 14th century; this time, the renewed prosperity came from trade with the colonies and, let's not try and hide the facts, from trade in "black ebony". Ships from Bordeaux carried arms, cloth and trinkets to kings of black tribes and exchanged them for slaves who were sold in the Antilles. The freight on the return journey consisted of sugar, coffee, cotton and indigo. This was a profitable trade which provided the town with immense wealth and, through the consequent intense activity in the harbour area, made Bordeaux France's foremost port on the eve of the Revolution.

The creation of the High Court, or Parliament, brought a whole new social class into being, and it had a major influence throughout the 17th and 18th centuries. The magistrates were the sons of wealthy merchants for whom the parents had purchased positions that carried titles with them and conferred a certain dignity on the bearer. These Presidents and Counsellors of the High Court or the Court of Aids (the equivalent of the Customs and Excise)

THE MASKS OF BORDEAUX

The masks that are a characteristic feature of architecture in Bordeaux, decorate numerous buildings and the ones on the waterfront are remarkable for their variety. The wide range of masks of people and characters usually show a contagious form of good humour and, with some justification, it has been said that the craftsmen who made them amused themselves by creating something for the pleasure of all who see them. The mask or mascaron (from the Italian *mascherone* meaning "mask") was already a decorative feature of mediaeval houses but it was in the 18th-century town that it was to become so commonplace and decorate mansions and residences. It was particularly in evidence on the waterfront buildings where each mask has its own personality; they are all different.

Starting from the Quai de la Monnaie, there is a continuous succession of unusual motifs right along the Quai Richelieu, then, further on, along the Quai des Chartrons. The same is true on numerous houses in the Chartrons District.

In the 19th century, masks continued to be carved on house fronts, e.g. on the house in the Rue Margaux where François Mauriac lived.

It is also said that, when the Maritime Exchange was built in 1924 as a replica of the Commodities Exchange, two of the masks included on the façade represented the Chairman of the Chamber of Trade at the time and the architect of the building...

THE PLACE DE LA BOURSE

This first breach in the mediaeval ramparts, commissioned by Intendant Boucher, was originally known as the Place Royale before becoming the Place de la Bourse. It was designed by the Gabriels, senior and junior, between 1730 and 1755 and was to provide a grandiose backcloth for a monumental statue of Louis XV. It also marked the birth of modern Bordeaux, as well as being one of the finest examples in the country of 18th-century French architecture. On one side is the Hôtel des Fermes (tax office), the first building to be constructed, while on the other is the Commodities Exchange. Between the two is a central pavilion. All the buildings are decorated with masks and pediments created by Verbeck, Van der Woort, Vernet and Francin.

Lemoyne's statue of Louis XV, which was unfortunately melted down in 1792, was replaced in 1869 by the Fountain of the Three Graces (a copy by Gumery of a piece by Visconti), said to represent the Empress Eugenia, Queen Victoria, and Queen Isabella II of Spain. What is certain is that the nudity of these gracious royal nymphs offended the prudish middle classes of the mid 19th century.

Inaugurated on 9th September 1749, the Commodities Exchange replaced the older Exchange but was still incomplete; work continued with the painting of the ceilings in the reception room (1752), later to be destroyed as a result of the fire caused by the air raids in 1940. The main staircase was also decorated and, in 1773, the wrought-iron gates were mounted, masterpieces of craftsmanship made by a locksmith named Dumaine. Wainscoting by Cabirol (1784) completed the interior decoration. The courtyard was open to the sky, so Bonfin covered it with a timber roof. Napoleon and the Empress Josephine inaugurated the new hall on 2nd August 1808 but, in 1865, Charles Burguet replaced the wooden roof and original lantern with cast iron rafters and a glass roof. This provided maximum light without detracting from the pure lines of the building as a whole. Finally, the same architect refurbished the Trade Court in a style that is very much "mid 19th century".

MUSEE NATIONAL DES DOUANES
1, place de la Bourse
10 am – 6pm – Closed Mondays
Tel.: 05 56 48 82 82

The Golden Age of a town made wealthy by colonial trade

were interested not only in political power (after all, they had stood firm against the king) but also in increasing their personal fortunes, which were by this time based on lands and property. Their vineyards were the subject of immense care and pride. It is to these powerful magistrate-wine growers that we owe the discovery of the art of producing and storing the great wines of the Médoc and Graves. Such were the Ségurs, who owned the châteaux of Latour, Lafite and Mouton, and the Pontacs who owned Haut-Brion. This was the reason for their staunch determination to uphold the commercial privileges enjoyed by the wines of Bordeaux that had existed since the days of the English occupation, and the President de Gascq gave a highly-significant answer to the governor, the Maréchal de Richelieu, when he stated, "Rest assured that the High Court would prefer to be annihilated than suffer wines to be brought down from the uplands!" As to Montesquieu, he congratulated himself on the success of his books because they provided publicity for the wine he produced in La Brède…

The preponderance of these "gentlemen of the Court" was to be found even in intellectual circles (although it is true that they possessed a remarkable degree of culture and erudition) when, in 1712, Louis XIV signed the letters patent that led to the creation of the Royal Academy of Science,

THE GRADIS MANSION (l'hôtel Gradis)
At the corner of Cours Victor-Hugo and Rue Sainte-Catherine is a mansion built in the mid 18th century for Abraham Gradis, one of the most famous members of Bordeaux' Jewish community. His family originally came from Portugal and had made its fortune as arms dealers in the 17th century. Abraham played an important role during the Seven Years' War – he gave the government fourteen ships, only one of which returned! After France had lost Canada, Gradis turned his attention to the French West Indies and Mauritius. For a while, he worked with Beaumarchais. He had access to the Court in Versailles and was on familiar terms with the Maréchal-Duc de Richelieu. A few days before he died, in his mansion, the aldermen gave orders that the Great Bell nearby should remain silent to avoid disturbing the "famous Jew, Gradis" during his last few hours.

Letters and Arts of Bordeaux. Montesquieu was to be its Rector a few years later and very quickly, most of the future magistrates attended it to be trained.

OPPOSITE
Built in 1869, the Fountain of the Three Graces marks the heyday of the city's urban development.

The Great Town Planner-Intendants

In the 18th century, the town also benefitted from a succession of great intendants who transformed and improved the community. Despite the unwillingness and penny-pinching of the local councillors,

THE STAIRCASE IN THE FONFRÈDE MANSION

This spiral staircase designed by Victor Louis for the mansion built for P.B. Fonfrède, the father of a well-known Girondin member of parliament, was revolutionary in its day. It was also famous outside Bordeaux – one foreigner even addressed a letter to "Mr. Fonfrède on his fine staircase in Bordeaux". The staircase is easily climbed and it is said that a rider once rode up it to the third floor.

Boucher, Tourny and Dupré de Saint-Maur succeeded in imposing their point of view, splitting the restrictive mediaeval ramparts and giving Bordeaux a complete facelift.

First and foremost came the Place Royale (now the Place de la Bourse), majestically set beside the river, the "most beautiful façade in the world". Then wide, tree-lined avenues were opened up, replacing the dark moats of the Middle Ages. Triumphal arches were built, and gates that were swirls of wrought-ironwork. A vast formal park was laid out in a town that had previously been devoid of any open spaces. The Place Dauphine (Place Gambetta) replaced a rubbish tip. Large houses were built with elegant balconies, and there were mansions, some of them truly sumptuous designs dating from a period immediately preceding the construction of Bordeaux' two gems – the Palais-Rohan commissioned by Monseigneur Mériadeck de Rohan, an Archbishop who loved opulence, and the Grand Theatre which was imposed on fearful councillors by a non-less opulent governor, the Maréchal-Duc de Richelieu. This was the veritable apotheosis of a town in which the wealth of architectural magnificence is a reflection of the fortunes invested in property with a fervour that was abruptly destroyed by the onset of the Revolution. The second half of the 18th century was the heyday of a pure Classical style of architecture whose refinement and harmony reflected the general joie de vivre. It was an architectural style that was to leave such a mark on the urban community that it became impregnated to an extent that seems to have created serious inferiority complexes among the town planners and architects of the following centuries… The Revolution and subsequent Empire caused a crisis from which Bordeaux found it difficult to recover. On the Place Dauphine (Place Gambetta), 302 heads were victim to the guillotine during the Reign of Terror. The Napoleonic Wars did little to encourage trade and it was hardly surprising that the people of Bordeaux were delighted at the return of the Bourbons and the monarchy. In a show of gratitude, the title of Duke of Bordeaux was bestowed on the heir to the throne and it was the poorest sections of society that celebrated the birth of the Duc de Berry's son with the greatest enthusiasm in 1820. Indeed, the "ladies of the market" clubbed together to buy a cradle for "their" Duke of Bordeaux!

THE GOBINEAU MANSION (l'hôtel Gobineau)
A mansion was erected in the late 18th century at the corner of the Cours du XXX Juillet and Allées de Tourny for a Councillor named de Gobineau (it was built by Durand to plans by Louis). Built with stone from the initial demolition work on the Château Trompette, this mansion was to be used as the basis for the alignment of the future Cours du XXX Juillet and as the starting point for the building of the eastern side of the Allées de Tourny in the 19th century. It was later given an additional two storeys, and has now become the "Bordeaux Wine Centre".

The sale of the land on which the Gobineau Mansion was built was part of a vast fraud set up during Louis XVI's reign by a Councillor in the Customs and Excise Office, the front man for the Controller General of Finance, Calonne. In 1785, he launched a property investment programme when the king gave his agreement in principle to the local people's demands for the demolition of the Château Trompette.

This highly complex operation, which involved the Master of the Treasury and caused the downfall of the architect Louis, fizzled out in the storms of revolutionary France, although not before the new Minister of Finance had time to revoke the concession granted to the swindlers.

THE AQUITAINE GATE (la porte d'Aquitaine)

When Tourny decided not to keep the mediaeval gates, he ordered the demolition of the one that used to stand at the southern end of the Rue Sainte-Catherine and had the four awful towers flanking the Gothic gateway replaced by a veritable triumphal arch designed by the talented Portier. Since then, this has become known as the Aquitaine Gate, in honour of the Dauphine's second son, the Duke of Aquitaine. On one side, the gateway is decorated with the royal coat-of-arms and maritime gods holding the shield; on the other are the town's coat-of-arms emerging from a cup being showered with fruit and flowers.

Made of fine stone from Saint-Macaire, with a central archway that is more than 36 ft.high and 16 ft. wide decorated with

projecting rustication, the Aquitaine Gate replaced the St. Julian Gate in 1753. The original gateway, dating from 1302, been named after a nearby hospital opened in 1231 to care for lepers and plague victims. It was used by travellers heading for Spain. Wickets had been designed for each side, to cater for the passage and control of pedestrian traffic.

It was in front of this gate that the market for produce from the Landes used to be held and, from the early 19th century to July 1841, people attended public executions on the square. They attracted the painter Goya during his visit to Bordeaux.

The Faculty of Medicine and Pharmacy was built between 1880 and 1914. Since 2005, a column designed by sculptor Ivan Theimer has stood in the centre of the square.

The Great Town Planner-Intendants

THE BURGUNDY GATE (la porte de Bourgogne)

It has been said that the Burgundy Gate dedicated to the Dauphin's son, the Duke of Burgundy, was "the apple of Intendant Tourny's eye". Completed in 1755, the veritable triumphal arch built by Portier was placed on a site overlooking the river at the end of the former moats leading to the Town Hall, then situated on what we now know as Cours Victor-Hugo. Later, when the first bridge in Bordeaux was built, just in front of the gateway flanked by the line of buildings along the waterfront, it became the most majestic gesture of welcome to visitors from the north. The construction of the gate posed problems that worried Tourny, but Gabriel, the architect, reassured him. "Portier", wrote Professor Pariset, "suggested inserting iron ties in the construction, the work to be carried out by Fuet… However, in order to avoid unnecessary extra weight, it was decided in 1755 not to include the carvings shown on the original plans. Despite this, the gateway is a fine piece of building." "We needed an architectural order", said Tourny, "and the Tuscan order had been used on other gates. We could do no better than to rise further, to the Doric. Anybody would think that he wanted to turn his town into a living museum of antique orders!"

It should be remembered that the Burgundy Gate replaced the former Salinières Gate in the 14th-century ramparts which was pushed ajar and quickly closed again "to those who arrived with the tide at night or who wanted to embark or who came from the landward side". In those days, the gates were closed at 8 p.m. on winter evenings and 10 p.m. in the summer.

When Napoleon came to Bordeaux in 1808, the gateway was hastily decorated – with painted wooden panels!

Moreover, before the Burgundy Gate was built, the town's aldermen had had the old moats (now Cours Victor-Hugo) improved by laying out buildings and by imposing on any new buildings erected after 1711 a unity that is particularly recognisable on the right-hand side of the road beyond the triumphal gateway.

THE MINT GATE (la porte de la Monnaie)

In 1758, this gate facilitated movement between the wharves and the Capucin District. The mint had been opened on an adjacent site in the previous year, hence its name. An elegant construction with a fine frieze and a cornice, it was one of a number of archways commissioned by Intendant Tourny to replace the mediaeval town gates. Here, though, the archway marked an entirely new opening in the ramparts rather than a replacement as in the case of the Dijeaux and Aquitaine Gates.

THE LALANDE MANSION (l'hôtel de Lalande) >

This mansion, which is a perfect example of the private residences built in the 18th century, was designed in 1779 by Laclotte for a Councillor named Raymond de Lalande. Nowadays, it houses the Decorative Arts Museum. The former reception rooms with their mahogany flooring, the dining room with its original wainscoting and the perfectly-preserved antechambers are the ideal setting for the presentation of regional 18th-century artwork (pottery, furniture, porcelain made for the French East India Company, gold artefacts, wrought-iron work, glass, silverware, and wood panelling from various Louis XV and Louis XVI mansions). All the refined elegance of Bordeaux's golden age can be seen here.

MUSÉE DES ARTS DÉCORATIFS
39, rue Bouffard
Tel. : 05 56 10 14 00 – Fax : 05 56 10 14 01
mailto: musad@mairie-bordeaux.fr
11 am – 6 pm (2 pm – 6 pm, Saturdays and Sundays)
Closed Mondays and public holidays
The museum of decorative arts houses collections of furniture, ceramics and gold or silver items in an 18th-century private mansion.

The Lalande Mansion.

Samadet faïence: pots with multi-coloured decoration.
Musée des Arts décoratifs.

< THE DIJEAUX GATE (la porte Dijeaux)

Inscribed in the pediment of this gate, constructed by Nicolas Portier between 1748 and 1750, is a decorative feature made by Francin (1753) – the town's coat-of-arms. This gate replaced the one that had been built some ten metres nearer what we now know as the Place Gambetta. Placed between two round towers in the 14th-century ramparts, it was preceded by a barbican that was itself covered by a moat. It was in front of this gate that the royal troops fought in 1650, during the Fronde Revolt.

The Great Town Planner-Intendants

A painting in the Musée des Arts Décoratifs: *View of the Quai des Chartrons* by Pierre Lacour (1804).

THE ART GALLERY (musée des Beaux-Arts)

Since 1881, the Art Gallery has been housed in specially-designed premises in the City Hall Gardens. It contains some three thousand works and the sheer number means that they have to be displayed on a rota basis. In the various rooms are admirable examples of 16th-century Italian paintings (Titian, Perugino), 17th-century works by Rubens, Van Dyck and Brueghel, 18th-century portraits by Nattier and Reynolds and still lifes by Chardin, and, in the 19th-century room, Delacroix' famous work *Greece on the Ruins of Missolonghi*. The rooms devoted to more modern artists not only contain works by Boudin and local artists such as Albert Marquet and Odilon Redon but also a recently-acquired oil by Picasso, *Olga Reading* (1920).

MUSÉE DES BEAUX-ARTS
20, cours d'Albret
Tel. : 05 56 10 20 56 – Fax : 05 56 10 25 13
E-mail : musbxa@mairie-bordeaux.fr
11 am – 6 pm
Closed Tuesdays and public holidays.

THE PALACE OF AN ARCHBISHOP, PRINCE DE ROHAN

From 1722 to 1778, Bonfin worked on the construction of a palace designed by the Parisian architect, Etienne, for Archbishop Mériadeck Monbazon, Prince de Rohan. Unfortunately for this ostentatious prelate, he never occupied the palace for it was completed after he had left Bordeaux. It was used as the Bishop's Palace, as county offices and, later, as the Prefecture. It became an imperial palace in 1808, a royal castle in 1814 and, since 1835, it has been the City Hall.

This austere, well-balanced palace has an Ionic portico in front of the main courtyard at the back of which is the harmonious façade with a pediment carved by Cabirol. Inside, note the magnificent salons, the dining room with its trompe-l'oeil paintings by Lacour, and the amazing stonework on the main staircase.

The palace housed the new County Council in 1790 and, later, the Revolutionary Tribunal. In 1800, it was the new Prefect, Thibaudeau, who was accommodated here, for the First Consul insisted that his representative should be given lodgings fitting to his function. One of his successors, Charles Delacroix, the "official father" of the famous painter, died here and, in 1808, the Emperor took over the palace.

In one fell swoop, the former Archbishop's Palace had been raised to an imperial palace, and the Prefecture was transferred to the former Saige Mansion. Less than seven years later, the white flag flew over the palace which had become a royal residence. The Duchess of Angoulême spent four months here in 1823 and, in 1828, it was the Duchess of Berry who stayed in the palace when she came to inaugurate the new St. Andrew's Hospital and lay the foundation stone for the rostral columns.

In 1833, the State offered to exchange the Rohan Palace for the Town Hall (on what we now know as Cours Victor-Hugo) which the Ministry of War wanted to turn into barracks. If the town refused, the palace would be used to accommodate the garrison. The negotiations were a long drawn out affair. It was not until 1835 that the exchange was made official and, on 1st January 1836, the Mayor, Mr. Brun, moved into the royal palace where, in 1839, the new Mayor, David Johnston, received King Louis-Philippe's eldest son, the Duke of Orleans.

Since that time, the town has continued to occupy the palace.

PALAIS ROHAN
Place de l'Hôtel-de-Ville
7 am – 8 pm from 01/04 to 31/10
7 am – 6 pm from 01/11 to 31/03
Tours on Wednesdays at 2.30 pm with advanced booking. Enter from Place de l'Hôtel-de-Ville.

TOWN HALL GARDENS
Cours d'Albret
7 am – 8 pm from 01/04 to 31/10
7 am – 6 pm from 01/11 to 31/03
The gardens lie behind the Town Hall, more or less on the site occupied by the gardens of the Archbishop's Palace in the 16th century. It was laid out in its present form in the 19th century, with a vast central lawn flanked by lime trees.

THE PLACE DU PARLEMENT

Laid out in 1754, the Place du Parlement is a harmonious, well-balanced design reminiscent of a theatre backdrop thanks to the building, in the 19th century, of houses in the same style as the ones that had been erected one hundred years earlier for Bordeaux' wealthy merchants.

The square has recently been paved and this adds to its overall charm, especially as the fountain placed in the centre in the mid 19th century provides a certain graceful elegance. Described as a "tormented piece of bric-a-brac", it is decorated with amusing female faces. It replaced the original fountain which was demolished in 1776 when the "royal market" was transferred

to the square. The market specialised in the sale of poultry brought down from the Saintes area by river barge. During the French Revolution, its name was changed to "Liberty Market". In the 19th century, some of the empty plots were built in the same style as the remainder of the square. This is known, in Bordeaux, as "architectural continuity".

The theatre has been given back the blues and golds that formed its decoration in the 18th century.

THE GRAND THÉÂTRE

Inaugurated on 7th April 1780 with a performance of *Athalie*, the Grand Theatre, which was the finest building designed by the architect Louis, stands on the site of the Gallo-Roman Tutelle Pillars, the forum in the 3rd-century city. Twelve Corinthian columns support the entablature on the peristyle that is, in fact, an audacious piece of building for it is held in place by a metal tie placed inside the construction, compensating for the enormous thrust from the flat vaulting. This invention has remained famous and is known as "Mr. Louis' nail". Above it are twelve statues by Berruer and Van Den Drix, representing the nine Muses, Juno, Venus and Minerva.

An elegant staircase with three flights of steps leads up to the first floor. It was copied by Garnier when he designed the Opera House in Paris.

For many years, there were shops beneath the galleries along the sides, including a café with a clay-floored terrace on the north side.

In those days, the theatre seemed to be half-hidden, dominated by the neighbouring buildings. Then, in 1846, an engineer called Thiac, son of an equally-famous father, decided that since the theatre could not be raised, the level of the surrounding ground would have to be lowered in order to show the building off in its full majesty.

Digging began on the Place de la Comédie, which made it possible to add a flight of steps in front of the theatre and avoid the unfortunate clashes of carriages and coaches which, until then, tended to hit the base of the columns so that they had to be protected with circles of wood and iron.

The lowering of the ground continued on Cours du Chapeau-Rouge then, in 1853, it was decided to lay out a slope along the incline of Rue Esprit-des-Lois with a square comprising lawns and flowerbeds. The arcades were closed off with balustrades, which unfortunately caused the final destruction of the last vestiges of the Tutelle Pillars.

The foyer and green room redesigned in the mid 19th century by Charles Burguet brought to this part of the theatre the richly-gilded decoration that was typical of the Louix XVI style as seen during the days of the Second Empire and that appears almost tawdry when compared to the remainder of the Grand Theatre where the genius of Louis created an atmosphere of ethereal elegance. The ceilings in the 19th-century foyer and green room were painted by Bouguereau, an artist from Bordeaux.

The mythological paintings cost 36,000 francs and it was said, severely but justifiably, that it was "cruel to set them next to true masterpieces, even if the desire to copy was honorable".

Since 1780, the Grand Theatre has undergone numerous alterations, some successful, others less so. They included the stage, which was altered to cater for technical innovations, and the auditorium modified in line with changes in taste. The passage of time was obvious. Hence the need for a restoration that, if it was to be satisfactory, had to lie somewhere between a return to the original layout and a continuation of the design of the building in 1989 when it was decided to begin a restoration project that was to cost one hundred and 30 million francs.

The work was to cover the foyer, cloakroom, main staircase, auditorium and all the stage machinery. The existence of numerous contemporary documents and the miraculous discovery of a sample of the blue colour chosen by the architect, Louis, enabled the project leaders to reconstitute the decoration in accordance with his original designs. During the mid 19th century, red was the favourite colour and it predominated from the entrance to the building right through into the auditorium; it was replaced by the original shade of blue magnificently set off by the decorative gilding. The stage curtain was patiently recreated and it was finally raised on 24th January 1992, revealing a stage in which the technologies of the past have been combined with those of the present and on which five hundred electrical circuits requiring 50 miles of cable are now operated from a central electronic control panel. In fact, in order to restore Louis' masterpiece to its original glory, high-tech specialists have combined with craftsmen whose skills have been handed down from days lone gone.

GRAND THÉÂTRE
Place de la Comédie. Tel. : 05 56 00 66 00
Guided tours are organised by the Tourist Office outside rehearsal times.

M. DE TOURNY'S PARK (le Jardin public)

In the middle of the 18th century, Intendant Tourny decided to give the people of Bordeaux a public park and a place for a stroll. He commissioned Gabriel, the architect responsible for the Place Royale (Place de la Bourse), to design a formal garden. It was laid out on what had previously been marshland and, after its inauguration in 1756, met with immediate popular success. During the French Revolution and the days of the Napoleonic Empire, however, this "meeting-place of merchants" suffered extensive damage. The gardens then lay abandoned for several decades until, in the middle of the 19th century, they were turned into an English-style park with serpentine river, island, tree-lined avenues and botanic garden. At the beginning of this century, the gardens acquired the "Petit Mousse" that is always followed by a procession of swans. It delights children just as much as the ever-popular Punch and Judy show. Stone statues of painters from Bordeaux (Carle Vernet, Rosa Bonheur) have decorated

the park for some years. Recently, they have been joined by a bust of the writer François Mauriac, made by Zadkine during the German occupation.

PUBLIC PARK
Cours de Verdun
7 am – 8 pm from 1st April to 31st May
7 am – 9 pm from 1st June to 31st August
7 am – 8 pm from 1st September to 31st October
7 am – 6 pm from 1st November to 31st March

NATURAL HISTORY MUSEUM
Hôtel de Lisleferme, Jardin Public
5 place Bardineau
Tel.: 05 56 48 29 86 - Fax: 05 56 01 28 59
mailto: museum@mairie-bordeaux.fr
11 am – 6 pm (2 pm – 6 pm Saturdays and Sundays).
The natural history museum contains a general zoological collection of specimens from all over the world. It also contains regional fauna and palaeontology.

When time stood still

With the coming of peace, business picked up again but Bordeaux was unable to regain its commercial prosperity of previous centuries and, after endless political storms, political power passed to the middle classes, a liberal but elitist group comprising Catholics, Protestants, and Jews, all of whom had been perfectly integrated into local society for almost three hundred years. Major town planning projects centred mainly on hygiene, the cleaning-up of districts that had changed little or not at all since the Middle Ages. This led, for example, to the laying-out of the Cours d'Alsace-Lorraine through a particularly evil-smelling district crossed by a polluted stream called the Peugue. And many of the narrow squalid streets were widened.

In 1822, a stone bridge was inaugurated, and at last there was a means of crossing the Garonne other than by boat. The consequence of this was that forty-three years later La Bastide was annexed to the town and the right bank underwent a period of expansion. Yet although hostility from some quarters had not prevented the arrival of the railway which was followed by a half-hearted attempt at industrialisation, the 19th century was the period "when time stood still", as Professor Guillaume described it. It was not until the second half of

The Galerie bordelaise, a fine example of neo-Classical architecture, designed by Gabriel-Joseph Durance in 1831 for the Marquis de la Torre.

the 20th century that major projects were again undertaken, with a view to bringing the town that had become the capital of Aquitaine right up to date.

BORDEAUX' UNDERGROUND STREAMS, THE PEUGUE AND THE DEVEZE

For several thousand years, two invisible streams have flowed through the city's subsoil. Both of them flow into the River Garonne after following a fairly complicated course. They rise in the sand, join each other then separate again before flowing into the river.

During violent storms in August, the Peugue and Devèze have always caused problems for the people living near them, mainly outside the line of boulevards encircling the city. In the Middle Ages, both of the streams would burst their banks along the section where they flowed as one between Cours d'Albret and Rue du Tondu, creating and maintaining marshes that were said to be the cause of plague. Cardinal François de Sourdis (1575-1628) made it a point of honour to fight this scourge by draining the marshes and, in their stead, laying out immense gardens flanked on all sides by canals. Rue du Marais ("Marsh Street") behind the Ornano barrack is a reminder of the old wetlands. The Peugue rises on the edge of the Landes plateau to the west of Pessac, in the "Bois des Sources" ("Springs Woodland"). It flows over a distance of some 12 kilometres until it reaches the Garonne. It used to flow in the open air throughout its course and was crossed by small plank bridges, called "*palanques*" in Gascon. The 1755 de Lattré plan shows the Peugue flowing in the open air as far as Rue Sainte-Catherine. Beyond that point, it flowed under the houses in a stone-vaulted sewer with fine bonding. However, the canalisation of the Peugue in 1868 sounded the death knell for the craftsmen and traders who had worked in the area since the Middle Ages. The tanners moved away, and tripe sellers and butchers no longer threw their waste into the river. The watermills stopped grinding corn beside St. Andrew's Cathedral. Like something from a Victor Hugo novel, the sewer still surreptitiously follows the line of Cours d'Asalace-et-Lorraine, forming a tunnel 4.80 metres wide and 3.30 metres in height. Under some of the buildings on this main thoroughfare, there are said to be trap doors through which small flat-bottomed boats called "*allèges*" used to be loaded and unloaded.

An eye witness recounted that, in the early 20th century, workers employed in the Ornano district still lowered their bottles of wine down into the Peugue to keep them cool.

More recently, when the houses along one side of Rue des Frères-Bonie were demolished, workers lifting the floorboards discovered the Peugue canal underneath.

The Peugue from the rue Dufau, 1854. Lithography by Légé.

The Devèze, an invisible presence in the town, is a modest tributary of the River Garonne but it played a more important role in the town's history than its brother, the Peugue, because it provided water for the channel through the ancient harbour. The stream is an anodyne little waterway at its source, at an altitude of 15 metres on the edge of the runway in Bordeaux-Mérignac Airport. It flows through Beaudésert, across the Bourran estate in Mérignac then along the Rue des Lavoirs and Avenue d'Arès. It crosses Boulevard Antoine-Gautier on a level with the old bus depot and follows the wall of the Carthusian cemetery. After flowing through the southern end of the Mériadeck district, it flows along Rue Elisée-Reclus and joins the Peugue on Place Rohan, in the main sewer that flows under Place Pey-Berland and Cours d'Alsace-et-Lorraine.

In 1925, during work on Rue Bouffard, the arch of a bridge was uncovered opposite No. 25, a reminder of one of these ancient streams.

Where does the Devèze get its name from? It may be derived from the Latin *divitae* meaning "wealth" or from Divona, the divine stream of the Gauls but this is all mere conjecture.

In 1970, an archaeological dig on Saint-Christoly Island revealed a set of timber and stone quays and constructions on the banks of the waterway, dating from the days of the Ancient Romans.

THE STONE BRIDGE (le pont de Pierre)

Getting across the Garonne had been a major problem for the people of Bordeaux for many a long year. The great intendants of the 18th century had devised numerous solutions, but building a bridge across a river more than 500 yds. wide and often in spate was a daring feat indeed. Until it was completed, people had recourse to ferrymen when, arriving from the north, they wanted to enter one of the largest towns in France. Imagine Napoleon's anger when he had to resolve this difficult problem for his troops who were then on their way to Spain to fight! Between 1st April 1809 and 18th April 1810, a wide variety of resources was placed at their disposal to enable the 181,131 footsoldiers, 43,986 mounted troops, and more than two thousand cannons and waggons to cross to the other side. So it was that, by a decree signed in 1810, the Emperor ordered the building of a wooden bridge.

Twenty-one years later, it was the governing body during the Restoration period that inaugurated – a stone bridge. On 26th August 1821, a toll bridge was opened for traffic. It was 527 yds. long and supported by seventeen arches faced with brick. It was designed by an Inspector General of the Highways Department, Claude Deschamps, and it suffered many ups and downs. First of all, there were technical problems; later, the difficulties were of a financial and political nature. It took the intervention of Lainé, a government minister who was born in Bordeaux, an energetic prefect named Tournon, and tradesmen in the town such as Balguerie-Stuttenberg and Daniel Guestier, to resolve the problem once and for all. They set up a private company which undertook the daring task at its own risk. However, the company was granted one compensation – the right to levy a toll (5 centimes for a pedestrian, 35 centimes for a horse and rider, and 70 centimes for a carriage).

It was not until 1st May 1822 that the new bridge, by then open to all traffic including carters, provided a real opportunity for La Bastide, part of the right-bank community of Cenon. The district was soon to enjoy industrial expansion, especially as it was in La Bastide that the first stations were built when the railway finally ran as far as Bordeaux.

The stone bridge brought La Bastide and Bordeaux so close together that, in 1865, the town received permission from the Emperor to simply annex this part of Cenon. It then became a district of the larger town without losing any of its own personality.

The Stone Bridge with the fire station on the right (1954),
an innovative design by architects Claude Ferret,
Adrien Courtois and Yves Salier.

When time stood still

LA BASTIDE, FROM COUNTRYSIDE TO INDUSTRIAL SUBURB

After belonging to the Church and feudal lords, the land along the right bank of the Garonne in Bordeaux slowly fell into the hands of traders and parliamentarian-winemakers. Marshland wines enjoyed huge success in those days. They were particularly full-bodied, with a good deep colour, and were better able to withstand transport by ship, even when the journeys were long. They were famous for their raspberry bouquet and were also known as "return wines" because of their use for the export trade. Among the most famous owners in Bordeaux were the Jewish banker Peixotto, Baron Sarget who promoted the passageway of the same name off Cours de l'Intendance, shipowner Adophe Balguerie, Blanc-Dutrouilh and poet Edmond Géraud who, in 1824, invited to his estate at La Belle-Allée fellow poet Alfred de Vigny who was then serving in a garrison in Bordeaux. The construction of the Stone Bridge in 1822 and the arrival of the railway in 1847 gradually changed the face of the right bank. The countryside was replaced by an industrial suburb and the vineyards were slowly replaced by timber plants, food and metalworking industries and shipyards. Between the hillside and the river an "industrial crescent" stretched from Les Queyries to Floirac-La Souys.

Yet the charms of this bank, which is still unspoilt in a few places, continue to appeal to people today.

The journal, *Le Producteur*, described a beautifully harmonious landscape, "The Cenon Hill is dotted with elegant country houses. From the hilltops, the view encompasses the entire Labastide plain with its thousand and one gaily-placed houses looking pretty and cool in the middle of their gardens and vineyards. Beyond that, the gaze takes in the majestic river covered with ships sailing under the flags of all the nations in the world and extends over the city developing so widely round the semi-circle formed by the river, a city in which the architecture shows such good taste, the streets are so wide

The Orléans Railway Station is now a cinéma.

The Community Centre in La Bastide was inspired by the Art Nouveau style and designed by architect Cyprien Alfred-Duprat. It was inaugurated in 1926. Its renovation, in 2005-2006, brought it back to the attention of numerous local people. © Assocation Pétronille.

The Blue Lion on Place Stalingrad, a work by sculptor Xavier Veilhan.

and the people so gracious in their manners. In short, from the hilltop, this is a visual paradise. Nowhere else in the universe can provide a more delicious sight."

La Bastide is blessed indeed, providing the people of Bordeaux with milk, eggs, wine and vegetables. It was also beneath its cool shady branches that the townspeople would come in large numbers in the summer, to breathe country air impregnated with the scents of the sea in its lush meadows, forgetting the work and stifling atmosphere of the nearby town. Young lovers could walk hand in hand along the picturesque Chemin du Rouquet (no longer in existence) through vineyards and marshes.

When time stood still

THE PLACE AMÉDÉE-LARRIEU

The tiny square named after Amédée Larrieu is a fine example of turn-of-the-century Art Nouveau. It lies off the usual beaten tourist track and is unknown to many locals yet both square and fountain are representative of the last couple of decades before the outbreak of the First World War. Amédée Larrieu was a former Prefect, and Member of Parliament for Gironde at the National Assembly in 1871. He had a son who died in 1896 at his home, Château Haut-Brion in Pessac, after bequeathing to the city of Bordeaux the sum of 150,000 French francs, part of which was to be used to pay for public fountain on the Place de Pessac, situated at the junction of Rue de Belfort and Rue de Belleville. The square was immediately named after Amédée Larrieu then, in 1897, a competition was launched to select a design for the fountain that was to erected on it. Twenty-three of the original fifty projects were short-listed and the first prize was eventually awarded to a sculptor named Verlet. At the top of the fountain is a female figure symbolising the Vine and filling the baskets of grape-picking cherubs. The remainder of the decoration consists of Tritons and fountains. The construction of the fountain did not go smoothly and it was not finally installed until 1902. It has now regained its original water-spout.

THE LAW COURTS (Palais de Justice)

Dominated by the statues of Malesherbes, Aguesseau, Montesquieu and l'Hospital, the Neo-Grecian peristyle of the Law Courts that were designed by the architect Thiac has stood on the Place de la République since 1846, opposite St. Andrew's Hospital built seventeen years earlier to designs by Jean Burguet.

The Courthouse was built over a section of the former Fort du Hâ. After the One Hundred Years' War, and Bordeaux' return to the kingdom of France, King Charles VII mistrusted the local population who were suspected of supporting the English cause and, in addition to having the Château Trompette built near the river, he installed the royal troops in a fort that was responsible both for controlling the town and keeping watch over the roads from the south. The Fort du Hâ was reinforced on many occasions until, during the Revolution, it became a State prison with some six hundred inmates.

In 1835, part of the fort was demolished. This left a vast empty space that was used for the Law Courts while the former military exercise yard was turned into a public square in 1844. Thus it was that the Place de la République was flanked by the Law Courts on one side and by the new St. Andrew's Hospital on the other.

As to the remainder of the Fort du Hâ, standing adjacent to the Courts, it continued to be used as a prison for many years; in fact, it was even used for capital punishment until the inmates were moved to the new model-prison of Gradignan and the National Magistrates' College was built in its place.

THE GIRONDINS' COLUMN (la colonne des Girondins)

When the Château Trompette was demolished, it was replaced by a vast esplanade – the Place des Quinconces. In the front are two rostral columns symbolising trade and navigation. At the other end of the square, in the centre of the semi-circle, is the Girondins' monument, erected in 1902.

The Girondins' Column marked the completion of a square covering some twelve hectares that had been rather slow to take shape since the solemn planting of the staggered rows of trees in January 1818 to embellish one section of the former site of the Château Trompette.

In fact, the trees were not all planted until 1835, many years after the erection of the rostral columns and the completion of buildings on each side of the esplanade. Their regular, identical façades had been designed shortly after the 1830 Revolution by architects Poitevin and Mazois.

Initially known as Place Louis XVI then Place Louis-Philippe, the new square was not given its final name until after the 1848 Revolution and the planting of a Tree of Liberty by the Mayor, Billaudel.

With the completion of the final stages of the Girondins' Column came the demolition of the Neo-Classical baths built on the side of the square during the Restoration of the monarchy.

Les Colonnes rostrales.

When time stood still

THE GIRONDIN HORSES

(les chevaux du monument aux Girondins)

When, at the end of the 19th century, the Girondins' Column was erected, it caused no end of controversy. Once the subject matter had been chosen (a glorification of the Republic), a decision had to be taken as to the best location for the column. Eventually, in 1888, a board reviewed some twenty-eight projects before finally retaining the one filed by the sculptor, Dumilâtre, who was to work with the architect, Rich. Together, they designed a column topped by figures of Genius and Liberty while, at the foot, they imagined a representation of "our illustrious compatriots", symbolical groups from which the Girondins were, in the final analysis, excluded! A town

councillor protested, "All these columns (he was also referring to the rostral columns) will turn the Place des Quinconces into a skittle alley!"

Yet the council's worries were by no means over. Difficulties arose when the earthworks were being undertaken (they revealed the foundations of the ancient castle, Château Trompette), costs spiralled and, of course, funding began to dry up.

Finally, at the dawn of the 20th century, the 140-foot column was built with, at its foot, sea-horses spouting water. Unfortunately for the horses, their bronze was an enormous temptation to the German occupying forces, who removed them in 1943. They were rediscovered, by chance, in Angers in 1945 and remounted on the fountain in 1983, much to the delight of the locals.

When time stood still

THE AQUITAINE MUSEUM

In 1867, the collection of artefacts from the days of Ancient Rome and Greece which had been built up during the period prior to the French Revolution became the Archaeology Museum. It was housed in the former Dominican Friary in Rue Mably. After a complete re-organisation in 1960, the exhibits were set out in the Rohan Palace Gardens but, two years later, the city extended the scope of the collections and opened the Aquitaine Museum, a vast display relating to regional history and ethnography.

Since 1986, the museum has been housed in the former Faculty of Arts on Cours Pasteur. Laid out in a manner that is as tasteful as it is instructive, the collections describe everyday life in Aquitaine from prehistoric times to the present day. A tour of the museum takes visitors from reconstructions of rock shelters containing masterpieces of Palaeolithic art to a description of the prosperous Gallo-Roman period (exhibits come from the digs carried out on Cours Victor-Hugo and include a statue of Cautopates, companion of the god Mithra and proof of the existence of this cult in the area in the 3rd century). The Middle Ages are represented in the form of sculptures (including the magnificent rose window from the Carmelite Church) and the Renaissance is not forgotten (Montaigne and his tomb). It is, though, Bordeaux's golden age (the 18th century) which offers the greatest number of truly superb exhibits.

As to life in the region's country districts, it is described in detail through models, reconstructions and a large collection of traditional farm implements. Finally, river boats and ships, life in lands afar and the city's colonial past are all remembered in the final collections relating to the 20th century.

MUSÉE D'AQUITAINE – 20, cours Pasteur – 11 am – 18 pm. Closed Mondays and public holidays. Mailto: musaq@mairie-bordeaux.fr. Tel.: 05 56 01 51 00 – Fax: 05 56 44 24 36 – Tel. groups: 05 56 01 51 04

Statue of Hercules, bronze.
2nd-3rd centuries.

« Le port de Bordeaux et le commerce avec l'Outre-Mer », 1925,
painting by Marius de Bozon.

L'Olivier: model boat.

Cautopates, companion of
Mithra: a statue uncovered
during an archaeological
dig on Cours Victor-Hugo.

When time stood still

"L'étalage" after Ferdinand Maröhn (19th century), a frontispiece for *Le Musée des Rieurs*. Lithograph by Victor Dollet, 1847, 49.6 x 37.2 cm. Bordeaux, Musée Goupil, inv. 96.I.1.285.
© Bordeaux Town Hall, photo by B. Fontanel

THE MUSÉE GOUPIL

The Goupil Museum contains the collection that once belonged to the House of Goupil, a dynasty of Parisian art publishers who worked from 1827 to 1920.

The collection includes 46,000 engravings, 70,000 photographs and 4,500 etched copper plates. Some are original works; others are reproductions of engravings or photographs. Together, they provide a panoramic view of 19th-century Art and tastes. They also give an insight into all the copy methods used at a time that was full of new inventions.

The collections in the Goupil Museum explain the first steps in the mass distribution of pictures on an international scale. They take visitors into the heart of the amazing world of images, just as they were beginning to circulate throughout the world.

The Goupil Museum has only temporary exhibitions. It is housed in the same building as the Aquitaine Museum at 20 cours Pasteur. Tel.: 05 56 01 69 40
mailto: musgoupil@mairie-bordeaux.fr

THE CHARTREUSE CEMETERY, "THE LAUGHING MEADOW OF DEATH"

The opening of the Père-Lachaise cemetery in Paris in 1804, designed by architect Alexandre Brogniard, offered a new idea of a cemetery as a place also designed for a stroll.

When author Stendhal came to Bordeaux in 1838, he was very impressed by the beautiful trees in the Chartreuse cemetery, the "laughing meadow of death". "Magnificent plane trees 40 to 50 feet in height form beautiful enclosures steeped in a great sense of melancholy." A few years later (1854), the Goncourt brothers were also delighted by this place overrun with "rose bushes that have a tendency to wander and roam like wild roses" and, in some places, by the "pale, ethereal greenery of a willow spreading its branches like the orderly hairstyle of a woman in tears".

Trees sometimes suffer a cruel fate. In 1942, the Town Council exchanged the beautiful plane trees (despite their reputation for having health-giving virtues) for oak timbers from which

to make coffins. The shortages meant they had little choice. One by one, the trees disappeared with the exception of a few old cypress trees that had survived since the beginnings of the cemetery. The annoying question of roots damaging the foundations of graves reappeared, as did the recurrent problem of dead leaves dirtying the graves and pathways. The problem was solved by a radical measure - 1,380 trees were cut down, including nettle trees, maples and sycamores.

In the 1950s, yews and lime trees were planted in place of the plane trees.

The Chartreuse cemetery, the "laughing meadow of death", was a moving sight indeed. The "garden of rest" had its own gardeners known as "*gazonniers*" and "*gazonnières*" and the name has survived to the present time to describe the people who maintain the graves.

Nowadays, the grass has disappeared from the squares and granite or marble tombs have taken over the smallest space. The cemetery has gained a "mineral" look. But along its pathways, there are still a few, dusty, distinguished old cypress trees and yews topiaried to give the graveyard the air of a formal French garden. Gradually, the cemetery is becoming a "garden of the soul", a pleasant place to get away from the noise and bustle of the city.

Open daily
Main entrance from Rue François-de-Sourdis and Place Gaviniès.
Guided tours arranged by the Tourist Office.
Tel. : 05 56 00 66 00

"ECHOPPES", HOUSES PECULIAR TO BORDEAUX

A characteristic feature of Bordeaux' urban landscape, the "*échoppe*" is the result of developments in housing. Originally, the word referred to a lean-to set against the walls of the mediaeval town. Later, in the 16th and 17th centuries, it was the name given to the shops of craftsmen or traders. By the 18th century, it had become a modest house built of limestone. It was mainly between 1860 and 1930 that it became a style of housing typically accommodating blue collar workers and the houses became increasingly common in the intermediate urban districts, in the area between the large 18th-century avenues and the city's boulevards. Later still, they could be seen in the inner suburbs, in Le Bouscat, Talence and La Bastide.

The single "*échoppe*" has a passageway to one side and three rooms opening off of it; a double "*échoppe*" has four rooms set out symmetrically. On the front, two windows next to a door on the side let light into two rooms overlooking the street. In some of the houses, a more or less noticeable basement includes a skylight that brings light into the cellar.

The façades, many of them extremely modest in appearance, may include a few discreet decorative features (cornices, cross-walls, keystones, moulded door or window frames and masks). Generally speaking, however, simplicity is the order of the day for "*échoppes*". Not that this prevents them from copying the bourgeois mansions standing next to them in some places and adorning themselves with carvings inspired by Art déco motifs or more Classical styles from the 18th century in Bordeaux and Art nouveau. There are thought to be 16,000 single-storey houses of this type here, making Bordeaux the largest French city, in area, for the size of its population.

What about the word "*échoppe*"? "*Echoppe*" or "*choppa*" appeared in legal texts at the end of the 15th century to refer to wooden lean-tos. In the southern French dialect, the langue d'oc, "*choppa*" meant a shop and, in old Gascon, "a gaol".

The keywords commonly used with "*échoppe*" are scullery, oilcloth, the dark room, foot scraper, veranda, courtyard, cloakroom and ground floor. The gardens of these houses are filled with windmill palms, bay laurel (sweet bay), privet, wisteria, vines, Atlas cedars, magnolias, cherry trees, pear trees, fig trees, banana palms and pomegranate trees.

AUSONIUS

Ausonius was born circa 310 A.D. and taught for 30 years at the University of Burdigala. He was then summoned to the court in Trier where he was tutor to young Gratian before becoming Prefect of the Gauls and, finally, Consul in 379 A.D. The poet from Bordeaux, who had a great love of his native land, died in 394 A.D. His writings are a precious source of information about the topography of Bordeaux and the surrounding area. Burdigala is described as follows, "Bordeaux is my birthplace. The sky is gentle and clement there; the soil is good and fertile, thanks to the rain. The spring is long and the winter mild as soon as the sun returns. The rivers ripple and flow so that, along the sides of the vine-clad hills, they seem to copy the ebb and flow of the tide. The square walls of the town form towers which are so tall that their tops pierce the clouds in the sky. Inside the town, there are well-traced roads, well-aligned houses, large squares worthy of their fame, gates that stand in line with the crossroads ..." There is no known picture of Ausonius. Only his traits of character, known thanks to his writings, have helped to create this portrait by sculptor Bertrand Piéchaud, a former student at the Ecole des Beaux-Arts (Art School) in Bordeaux and Toulouse. Ausonius is shown here in an official costume that is a reminder of his political functions. The bronze bust stands at the corner of Cours d'Alsace-et-Lorraine and Rue Ausone.

THE STATUE OF MONTAIGNE

When the Place des Quinconces was laid out in 1834, a public subscription was launched with a view to erecting a statue of Montaigne and another of Montesquieu. However, there was insufficient support for the project and it was not until 1858 that the admirable two sculptures by Maggesi were finally in place. One of them represents Montaigne, former Counsellor to the Bordeaux Assizes, a descendent of merchants who had acquired considerable wealth from trade in salt fish and woad, the Eyquems. After they had purchased the aristocratic estate of Montaigne, they took the name Eyquem de Montaigne.

In 1572, Michel Eyquem de Montaigne jotted down notes and his innermost thoughts while living in retirement in his "library" on his estate in the Dordogne. He exchanged countless letters with his friend, La Boétie, and, in 1880, finally published his *Essays*. One year later, he became Mayor of Bordeaux, which did not prevent him increasing his literary output and, by 1588, he had published three books.

From his travels, he returned with a «Journal» which confirmed his way of life and his style of thinking – the relativity of all things human, a philosophy based on wisdom, common sense and tolerance. These were the same ideas that Montaigne attempted to bring to the fore when he was Mayor of Bordeaux, on two occasions, between 1581 and 1585.

THE STATUE OF MONTESQUIEU

One of the statues on the Place des Quinconces created by the sculptor Maggesi in 1858 honours one of Bordeaux' most famous sons – Montesquieu. Charles de Secondat, Baron de La Brède, was born in 1689 in the château of the same name on the outskirts of Bordeaux where he was to write his delightful *Persian Letters* in 1721 before publishing his *Reflections on the Causes of the Grandeur and Declension of the Romans* (1734) and his most important work, *The Spirit of Laws* (1748) which was the one that brought him fame.

He was a Counsellor to the Bordeaux Assizes and one of the first members of the young Academy of Science, Letters and Fine Arts founded in 1712, an institution which he charmed by his encyclopaedic knowledge.

In 1726, he sold his office of President after having been elected to the Académie Française. He then travelled throughout Europe, spending some time in England where he studied an ideal democracy. It took him twenty years to prepare his «Spirit of Laws», a masterpiece of libertarianism and wisdom that was to inspire the authors of the Constitution in 1791.

It has been said that this "Lycurgus of Bordeaux would now be the ideal sage for the Europe of the Common Market". The sage of La Brède still inspires our thinking and forms the basis of studies, theses and longer works…

FRANCOIS MAURIAC AND BORDEAUX

He was "from here and from nowhere else", the young François Mauriac who was born at 86 Rue du Pas-Sant-Georges in Bordeaux on 11th October 1885. And it was in the midst of the noises and perfumes of a town quivering with passion and enthusiasm, close to a harbour on the banks of its river, in a town that people leave because its conservatism counters any attempt at creativity, that François Mauriac became aware of, and sensitive to, life.

When separated for even an instant from his mother, Claire Mauriac, as pupil in the kindergarten in Rue de Mirail far from the "bedroom decorated with grey", the young schoolboy was overcome with a sadness only children can feel. Yet this trying time was to be the source of much inspiration.

Neither the rigorous education dispensed by the Marian fathers in the "college opposite" and in Grand-Lebrun nor the climate filled with Catholic devotion and bourgeois decency succeeded in preserving him from the dichotomy between a love of the world and the love of God, the main feature of his life.

Having passed the nodal point that separates childhood and adolescence, François Mauriac moved from Rue Vittal-Carles to the old mansion in Rue Margaux and for the first time glimpsed the river glistening with a form of hope. "Sail away, leave Bordeaux and bid farewell to his adolescence". In 1907, he left Bordeaux for Paris and said goodbye to his adolescent years.

And when time moved forward

In a town where trade had been the main activity for so many years, industry was only gradually accepted, although it finally carved out its rightful place thanks, in particular, to high-tech. companies. As to town planning projects, they did not reach their full dimension until after 1960 and, in 1966, they led to the setting up of an Urban District (CUB) comprising the towns and villages from the entire metropolitan area. While Bordeaux was undergoing its economic transformation, it was also modernising its urban infrastructure. The Grand Parc was created, as was the Quartier du Lac with its Exhibition Centre. The universities were transferred to the suburbs, the central, but squalid, Mériadeck District underwent restoration and its 20 hectares became the town hall district with local authority and government buildings, offices, hotels and housing built around the only open space to have been created in the heart of a French town since 1914.

A preservation area of 150 hectares was also defined within which the 5,000 buildings, many of them already restored, regained something of the elegance of the "grand century" with the laying out of pedestrian precincts.

Finally, there was the opening of the vital ring road, freeing the riverside roads along the left bank of their heavy traffic. The harbour was transferred to the opposite bank and an outer harbour was developed in Le Verdon. Two additional bridges were built across the Garonne, including the Aquitaine Bridge which, since 1967, has presented an elegant outline more than 162 ft. above the waters of the river below, and the François-Mitterrand Bridge in the south of Bordeaux.

THE AQUITAINE BRIDGE (le Pont d'Aquitaine)

A daring construction slung 172 ft. above the Garonne at high waters, the Aquitaine Bridge (sometimes known as "Super-Tancarville") has a superstructure more than 735 yds. long extended by a viaduct over half-a-mile in length. The bridge as a whole rests on a veritable forest of 1400 concrete piles. In all, 140,000 cubic meters of concrete and 17,000 metric tonnes of steel.

This magnificent bridge, which was the brainchild of Bordeaux' mayor, Jacques Chaban-Delmas, is the result of a long effort that began in 1955 and that was aimed at catering for the expected increase in the flow of traffic north-south to and from Spain and the Garonne Valley. It was also designed to enable through traffic to avoid the centre of Bordeaux where it was blocking the stone bridge that was one hundred and fifty years old and that was, at that time, the only road across the Garonne. Not to mention the risks of obstruction and massive pollution within the town (this occurred on several occasions for there were sometimes as many as 7,000 vehicles an hour crossing the bridge!).

The daring enterprise and the problem of financing it (the bridge was to cost almost 150 million francs) took some time to resolve. Because of this, the Mayor of Bordeaux had to wait for the construction of «Super Tancarville» and, in the meantime, order the building of another bridge next to the railway line. It was called the Saget Bridge and, later, St. John's Bridge. It was inaugurated on 4th April 1960 and it drew off traffic heading for some of the suburbs on the right bank and for l'Entre-Deux-Mers. That evening, thousands of people danced on the newly-opened bridge…

Work began on the Aquitaine Bridge in 1960. It was finally linked to the northern motorway which had slip roads to the harbour areas of Ambès and Bassens as well as to the new North-Bordeaux District and its lake, and was inaugurated on 6th May 1967.

THE LONGEST WALL OF PLANTS IN THE WORLD
SQUARE VINET

Patrick Blanc is not unknown to the general public. Nicolas Hulot's TV programme, *Ushuaïa*, has given an insight into the character and talent of the agronomist and botanist who has such a love of woodland and tropical plants. He was first noticed in 1994 during the Festival of Chaumont-sur-Loire when his concept of a vertical garden offered a solution to the problem of gardens in densely-populated urban areas. As to the "wall of plants", it takes up very little ground area; in fact, it is quite the opposite to the traditional garden which requires a great deal of space.

The principle behind it is very simple and is based on three elements. A metal structure covered in PVC is given a layer of 3 millimetre thick nylon felt and pockets which enable the roots of plants to spread without the need for a natural substrate.

The "wall of plants" on Square Vinet is the largest ever created. Until it was erected, the square was frequented by children and a few locals but now it has become a "must see" for people enjoying a stroll and for tourists in search of the more unusual. The overall layout was provided by town planner and landscape gardener Michel Desvignes, the designer of Bordeaux' "Green Plan". A children's play area completes the new "garden of Eden" between Rue du Cancéra and Rue Maucoudinat.

THE RUE SAINTE-CATHERINE   >

The Rue Sainte-Catherine, which is over half-a-mile long, is one of the oldest streets in Bordeaux. It was, in fact, the great north-south Roman road or *cardo maximus* which, in the Middle Ages, was divided into several sections, some of them more winding than others but all of them bearing different names. It was in the 13th century that the name "Rue Sainte-Catherine" first appeared, and it referred to a chapel founded by the Knights of St. John of Jerusalem and dedicated to the holy martyr of Alexandria (the chapel was demolished in 1835 but stood on part of the site now occupied by the FNAC).

Originally, the name was given to the section of road between the Rue Porte-Dijeaux and the Place Saint-Projet, for the part between the Place de la Comédie and the Rue Porte-Dijeaux was known as the Rue Porte-Médoc, while beyond the Place Saint-Projet were the Rue de la Banquerie (where the butchers had their shops) and the Rue Marchande, then the Rue du Poisson-Salé, the Rue du Cahernan (between the Rue des Ayres and the Cours Victor-Hugo), the Rue Bouhaut (in the 16th century, home of the Jews who had been forced out of Spain and Portugal by the Inquisition), and, finally, the Rue Saint-Julien or Rue d'Aquitaine which led to the gate of the same name.

In the 19th century, all the streets were realigned as they had been in the days of the pax romana and, thereafter, there was only one, straight street, this time called Rue Sainte-Catherine. For the past few years, it has been a pedestrian precinct.

And it is still the busiest and liveliest street in the town.

FOLLOWING PAGES
Aerian view of the Place Pey-Berland,
St. Andrew's cathedral, the Town Hall,
and the buildings of the Magistrates' Court.
Photo by Jean-Jacques Saubi.

And when time moved forward

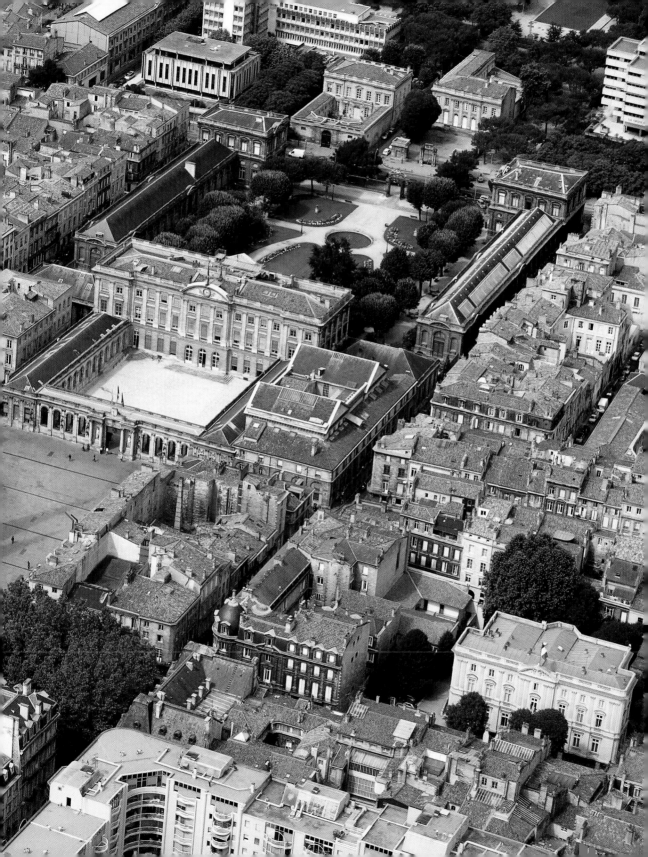

MICHEL CORAJOUD'S LANDSCAPED QUAYSIDES

Landscape gardener Michel Corajaud has installed his colourful flowerbeds and trees along the quaysides. The renovation of the quays will eventually cover a strip 4 kilometres long with an area of almost 40 hectares. The park alone on the banks at Saint-Michel will cover an area of 5 hectares, the same area as the public park.

When completed, this enormous green parchment will make the riverside area of the city more pleasant, especially during summer heatwaves.

The Prairie des Girondins opposite the Place aux Quinconces flanks Place de la Bourse, creating a garden of light and water and echoing the former Place Royale, a thin sheet of water moving like the tides and combining, "the sky, buildings and people in apparent depth". The main attraction of this vast green area will be the Garden of Lights, a sort of active landscape with a series of narrow gardens requiring only frequent mowing and cutbacks to accelerate the natural growth process. On Quai des Chartrons, the broken lines of trees produce a syncopated rhythm and a delightful play of light and shade, a sequence of areas of different dimensions and intensity.

It has been decided to include a wide variety of trees e.g. rowans, green oaks, medlars and maples chosen for their density and others such as hornbeam, Japanese zelkova, Chinese mahogany, nettle trees and tulip trees for their cool, thick shade. In front of the architectural façades, it was decided to plant trees with less compact foliage producing less dense shade e.g. laburnum, Judas-trees, yellowwood and mimosa which provide dappled shade without concealing the 18th-century façades.

And when time moved forward

Exhibition in the nave of the CPAC. Richard Serra, *Threats of Hell*, 29th June 1990 - March 1991

THE ENTREPÔT LAINÉ

This magnificent warehouse is a superb example of harbour architecture in the early 19th century. Showing as much attention to detail here as in the Stone Bridge, engineer Claude Deschamps oversaw the work from 1822 to 1824. Thanks to its historic monument listing in 1973 and its purchase by Bordeaux City Council from the Chamber of Commerce & Industry, the building was miraculously saved from destruction. Between 1984 and 1990, architects Jean Pistre and Denis Valode restored it and the interior layout was commissioned from Andrée Putman. It provides an exceptional setting for exhibitions organised by the CAPC Musée and the Arc-en-Rêve Association.

CAPC MUSÉE D'ART CONTEMPORAIN
7, rue Ferrère – Tel. : 05 56 00 81 50 – Fax : 05 56 44 12 07
mailto: capc@mairie-Bordeaux.fr
11 am – 6 pm (to 8 pm on Wednesdays). Closed Mondays and public holidays.

BORDEAUX' NEW BOTANIC GARDENS

Since the beginning of the 17th century, Bordeaux' botanic gardens have constantly moved from one location to another as opportunities arose and as required by changes to town planning.

In 1997, it was decided that it should be laid out in La Bastide, opposite Place de la Bourse. The site that it occupies today provided a chance to create numerous different views of the city, from various angles. France had not seen such a major botanic garden project for 25 years. The design was commissioned from architect-landscaper Catherine Mosbach and architect Françoise-Hélène Jourda.

Its innovative design breaks with the traditions of Classical botanic gardens based mainly on plant classifications. Ecology, sustainable development and education are the principal aims of the gardens in Bordeaux.

The gardens are divided into six landscape-worlds: a field of crops covering 44 plots; a gallery of typical regional environments; a pioneers' path with a structure based on piles of timber colonised by plants; an avenue of plants, where lianas and vines have pride of place; greenhouses; and, last but not least, the water garden displaying collections of water lilies and aquatic plants.

An arboretum contains a collection of tree leaves and bark. Allotments for local people give them a chance to share the joys of gardening and exchange tips.

JARDIN BOTANIQUE ET SERRES
Quai de Queyries
Tel.: 05 56 52 18 77
Fax: 05 57 14 23 40
Open 8 am – 8 pm
from 1st April to 31st May and 1st September to 31st October
8 am – 9 pm from 1st June to 31st August
8 am – 6 pm from 1st November to 31st March

And when time moved forward

The "miroir d'eau" in front of the place de la Bourse.

"Bordeaux reinvented"

Since Alain Juppé became Mayor of Bordeaux in 1995, the urban landscape has undergone extensive change. In fact, it is not unreasonable to describe Bordeaux today as a city that has undergone a metamorphosis.

Quaysides, squares, avenues and entire districts have been upgraded as a result of numerous face lifts, giving Aquitaine's capital back its erstwhile beauty. So many historic buildings have been brought back to their original splendour that it is difficult to count them all. Squares have been floodlit; the river banks redesigned with gardens and promenades. There are pedestrian precincts, cycle tracks and new locations designed for people to get together in convivial surroundings.

The design of the quaysides was the major feature of the great urban project because it re-established contact between the townspeople and the river, the Garonne, the natural central axis around which the bustling city centre has now developed.

Respecting the magnificence of the 18th-century "frontage" was the first requirement in the plans to upgrade the quays. This led landscape gardener Michel Corajoud and his team to use the expression "gardening the quays" i.e. using the art of gardening to lay out this long strip of public land where pedestrians, cyclists, tram passengers and cars each have their places.

The pond in front of Place de la Bourse, the special events and the play areas on Quai des Chartrons complete the project, as do the new outdoor dining areas. At the same time, the right bank has been given new amenities such as the botanic gardens, the universities and La Bastide housing development.

Bordeaux' tram, which won a prize for its innovative design, is another structural element – and a world first for its electricity supply, which has been undergrounded to remove the need for overhead lines and hanging wires over a distance of more than 10 kilometres through the heart of the historic old town. The tram has finally fulfilled the wish for a form of transport that respects the urban environment.

In just a few years, Bordeaux has also become a festival city with events such as *L'Escale du Livre* (books), the *Festival des Jardins* (gardens), the *Summer Festival*, the *Fête du Fleuve* (around the river), the *Fête du Vin* (wine) etc.

The city has other projects for the future including the building of a lifting bridge that would enable cruise liners to access the Port de la Lune.

The architectural quality of the city's heritage buildings led to Bordeaux being selected for inclusion in UNESCO's World Heritage list as an example of an outstanding urban environment.

INDEX

TABLE OF CONTENTS

TOURIST INFORMATION

Tourist Office - city centre
12 cours du XXX-Juillet
33080 Bordeaux Cedex
Tel. 05 56 00 66 00
Website: www.Bordeaux-tourisme.com
mailto: otb@Bordeaux-tourisme.com
9am - 7 pm (high season)
9 am - 6 pm (low season)
> Guided tours of the city, daily at 10 am
> Seeing the city district by district: Tuesdays, Thursdays, Fridays and Saturdays at 2.30 pm
> Shop with souvenirs and books about the city.

Tourist Office - Railway station
Gare Saint-Jean
Tel. 05 56 91 64 70
9am - 7 pm (high season)
9 am - 6 pm (low season)

Bordeaux Monumental
Tourist Office showcase for Bordeaux' heritage
28 rue des Argenters
Tel./Fax: 05 56 48 04 24
10 am-1 pm; 2 pm-6 pm from 01/11 to 30/04
9.30 am-1 pm; 2 pm-7 pm from 01/05 to 31/09
Located in the heart of Bordeaux old town, in the Saint-Pierre district, "Bordeaux Monumental" has

a permanent exhibition on Bordeaux with its old buildings, its history and its future.
> Multimedia exhibition
> Interactive book (unrestricted access)
> Learning about heritage for children and school pupils
> Conferences, talks, boutique etc.

Table

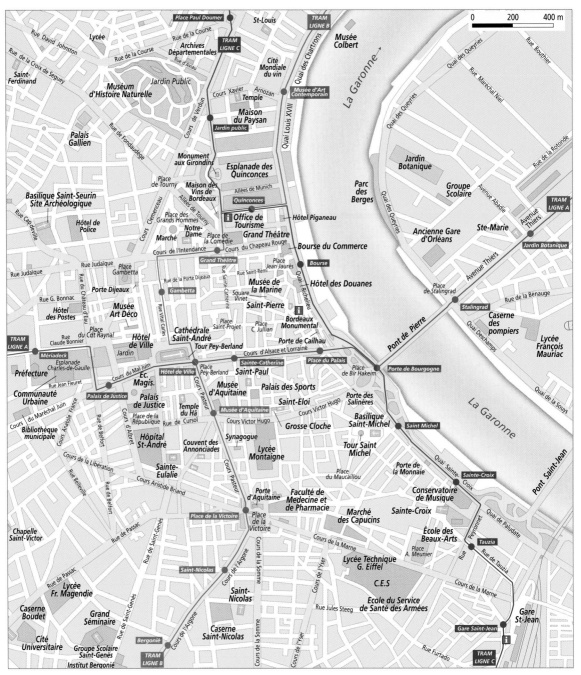

Map Patrick Mérienne

© 2007, Éditions Sud Ouest

This book was printed by Pollina in Luçon (85) – France. Photogravure by Labogravure in Bordeaux (33).

ISBN : 978-2-87901-787-7 – Éditeur : 22968.02.03.05.11 – N° d'impression : L57254